CATERPILLAR DREAMS

haiku

Rodney "Nova Sky" Mosley

Cover and interior illustrations by Lilia Zavada
Cover design by Michael Scott

Rodney T. "Nova Sky" Mosley
@novaskyzone

Printed in the United States of America

First Printing: June 2019

For the man who molded my being, my late loving father, Louis Leo Mosley.

For my best friend, bro, and editor Michael Scott. Without you, this book wouldn't exist.

For all the people out there facing chaos, I promise you, patiently embrace it and peace will be found.

Life is good and fun to live.

—LOUIS LEO MOSLEY

thoughts of you spark grief

love we shared incites progress

Pops, I'll make you proud

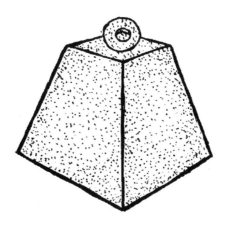

excuses of mine

weigh heavy on my conscience

remove them for flight

hurting those that love

chasing those that are broken

reasons he's alone

the dark void beckons

self-hate pleads for my return

my defiance holds

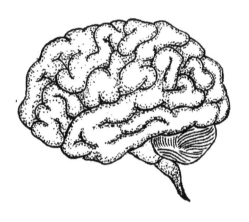

erratic thoughts form

daily, both best friend and foe

my ADHD

uncaged bird takes flight

a feeling so serene. oh

how I envy you

calming wind's touch soothes

my ragingly anxious heart

mother nature's love

glorious sunrise

signifies a fresh clean slate

make today the day

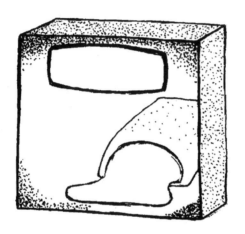

forged in the earth's core,

it's not hot magma, it's a

just-nuked Hot Pocket

first date's going great.

she tells me, I'll be right back

an hour has passed

your life's passions are

meant to heal you, not harm you

nurture your talents

my poisoned heart pleads

for your healing toxic touch

love's war with logic

sixth grade and pregnant

father's visits were nightly

men claim it's god's will

black teen felt depressed

prideful family ignored signs

funeral's next week

birthed from ashes of

the past, my soul's phoenix soars

life's demons cower

rich man asked poor man

why he was so damn happy

"because I'm alive"

corrupted beliefs

youth molded by tampered faiths.

indoctrinated

embrace aging, for

with it comes wisdom, and with

wisdom comes freedom

translucent stories

cloud my mental plane. I write

to clear the valley

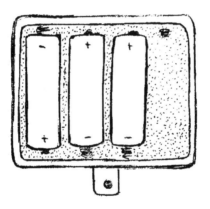

spark jolts my heart. it's

her. true love's creation, my

heart's lost battery

rhythmic muse, my love...

may we dance the tango of

our hearts connection

none above and none

below you, this class system

of lies breeds false pride

you tore me down in

hopes I'd quit, but all you did

was make me stronger

my soul. I've found her.

sitting at my heart's meadow,

her smile reflects life

pride burns within the

core of the hypocrite's heart

fueling their demise

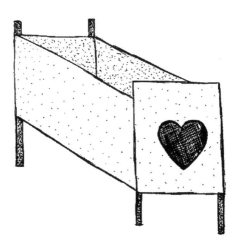

toddler loves bedtime

first class trip around the world

fly high young dreamer

alone with a good

book. soulful wind flows with love

sunlit afternoon

starlit wings carry

my resting soul to worlds far

celestial dreams

the past is the past

I want to move on, but our

love's memories don't

Cupid cried as my

love walked away. bittersweet.

his arrow had failed

black boy it's ok

to smile to cry to want love

the best you is you

nostalgic cartoons

trigger the purest laughter

let's never grow up

what makes you special

aren't the things you hold dear

it's the fact you're here

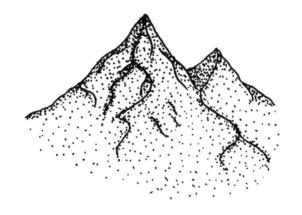

climbed up the mountain

almost got caught in the rain

missed a good challenge

beaming star behind

the clouds, molding our shadows

warming life's darkness

treat all of your crafts

with respect. that's the only

way they will blossom

record player slows

voices moan in love's chamber

her climax replays

shifting clouds flowed with

the strong wind. my hair joined in

I wish I could too

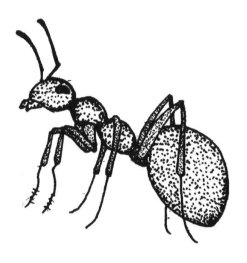

little ants lost their

way. stick blocks their current path

I'll help, small buddies

warm sunrise whispered

hello to the horizon

cloudy peekaboo

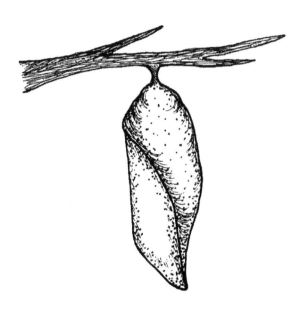

caterpillar dreams

of flight, cocoon calmly sings

patience, little guy

love, I long for our

past. can't force it, can't move on

can we try again

annoyed mall workers

procrastinator's best day

christmas eve shopping

faux leaders contort

a faith to fit their bias

truly blasphemous

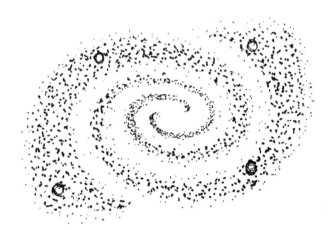

connected as one

within the Milky Way's womb

our hearts burning bright

choices I've made glare

back at me. challenging me

to focus on growth

I love you but my

actions are proving that I've

never loved myself

our talks under the

night's starry sky felt endless

those stars have fallen

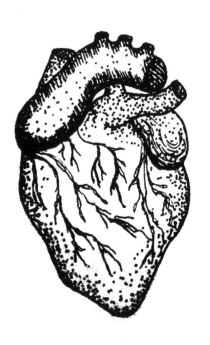

seven billion hearts

and mine beats only for yours

purest love of all

life's regrets tirade

against my substantial flaws

fueling my hunger

sun-pierced cloudy sky

brown leaves waltzing with the wind

nature's tranquil scenes

trainer prepped diet

I ignored it for pizza

live without regrets

we're a blip in time

compared to the universe

makes stress feel pointless

nature's morning hymns

reignite my soul each day

perfect alarm clock

life's like a chess game

a pawn can take out the king

outwit and persist

winter's cooling hold

mends the burn from summer's kiss

I still long for you

forgiving your past

allows your present to bloom

makes your future bright

our love's memories

made it hard to say goodbye

we kissed one last time

collapse on the couch

remote leaps across the room

wish I had children

once again we try

comfort doesn't equal love

once again we fail

spring night's calm, mood set

she moans I want you. we breathe…

loud cicada sings

voicemail. he called her

seeking comfort in her voice

her heart has moved on

storms of creation

crashed with passion through the night

our lust matched their strength

queens of power are

placing the kings in checkmate

patriarchy burns

egotistical

boasting only shows weakness

silence is power

petals of life have

guided me to your heart's core

true love's rose garden

mountains cry red tears

of anger for their Mother

man will feel their wrath

healer of my wounds

smile always brightens my soul

remembering her

young bird wants to fly

keeps falling, yet it still tries

please teach me your ways

pizza rolls feed my

soul. wait, I've eaten them all

life loses meaning

homemade Oreo

cheesecake. joy personified

heaven in each bite

worker ant now sick

of its norm, breaks the path that

society formed

faux leaders parade

their lies to fortify the

nation's great divide

broken cerebral

voices citing negatives

hindering my growth

before I judge the

stranger's life I ask myself

who the fuck am I

foggy mist blankets

the horizon. sun beams through

mirroring your heart

driving nowhere fast

the rampant speed of mankind

embrace the moment

some people call it

quits before they've even tried

how sad they must be

dragons ignite the

skies with radiating rage

my spirit's fury

god omnipotent

very easy to locate

look in the mirror

what is perfection

to the world it's what's trending

but to me it's you

puppet-stringed bigots

core of the one-percent's lie

blocking their hearts' peace

their complacent hearts

rotted their bond's foundation

loving a stranger

my soul's armor lies

before me, broken from war

I'm stronger without

money, hollow tool

that drives the man's heart to rot,

useless to the dead

young boy starts to cry

family laughs and says man up

toxic seed planted

blinding morning fog

blankets the land in silence

nature's quiet time

white teacher lost keys

asked black child to search dumpster

my first racial scar

love's burning ashes

suffocated her heart's strength

to love another

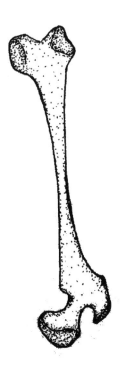

as time ages my

bones to brittle, my inner

child will remain strong

her soles caught fire

as the beat moved her to dance

the darkness away

ignorance blocks time's

wisdom. growing older while

still remaining lost

your tainted rose pricked

my heart's sensitive soul. now

it fears the garden

playing it safe gets

you nowhere. a bird that won't

leap will never fly

one's self-worth can't be

formulated by the world

only you know you

I pushed you away

because my toxic heart feared

you'd always love me

insecurities

flaws we assume others judge

no one gives a shit

mask of conforming

subliminally plastered

break it and be free

morning walk with her

she pulls me closer for warmth

priceless memory

those that don't try mock

those that do. definition

of the true failure

moonlight's smile cascades

across winter's darkened sky

warming its cold soul

society's pace

is a race to nothingness

every second counts

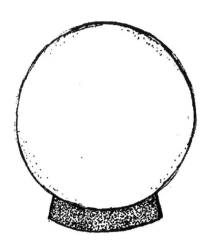

unspoken feelings

spark nothing but love's regret

no heart is psychic

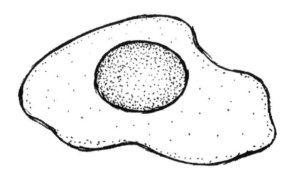

mother bird skips her

meal to satiate hatchlings

love takes sacrifice

yellow sun and moon

two souls linked by gravity

a love I long for

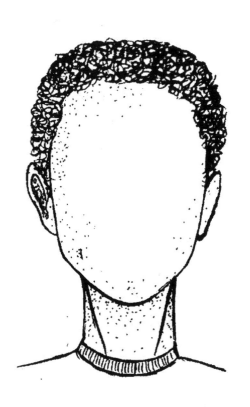

tears rain from son's eyes

his hero has taken flight

life's hardest goodbye

jungle's heart beats to

the drum of tranquility

Gaia after man

twenty-four seven

U.S. labor principle

working hard to die

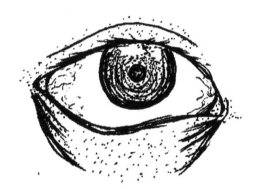

lost I lie alone

damp with tears from dreams of us

before you loved him

I'm addicted to

her toxic wine, my loveparched

heart drinks every time

old push mower, no

gas no plug just elbow grease

fine sunday morning

until you exhale

your last, your dreams are alive

in time they will fly

Made in the USA
Middletown, DE
30 January 2025